Chopin Masterpieces
for Solo Piano
46 Works

FRÉDÉRIC CHOPIN

DOVER PUBLICATIONS, INC.
Mineola, New York

Bibliographical Note

This Dover edition, first published in 1998, is a new compilation of works originally published in 1894 and 1895 by G. Schirmer, New York, in separate volumes of Schirmer's Library of Musical Classics under the group title *Frédéric Chopin/Complete Works for the Pianoforte.*

Carl Mikuli's full-length German *Vorwort* [Foreword] first appeared in Fr. Kistner's original publication of the Mikuli edition, Leipzig, 1879. The edited translation that has been adapted for the present publication appeared in Book XI [Sonatas] of Schirmer's Chopin series, 1895.

The Dover edition adds new headings as well as dates of composition based on primary sources. Popularized subtitles are included as familiar references; they appeared neither in the composer's manuscripts nor in early editions of the music. The composer's extensive dedications to patrons and students have been omitted in this edition. They appear in Dover's six-volume set of Chopin's music for solo piano.

International Standard Book Number: 0-486-40150-2

Manufactured in the United States of America
Dover Publications, Inc., 31 East 2nd Street, Mineola, N.Y. 11501

CONTENTS

As Chopin's student and, later, his teaching assistant, Karol (Carl) Mikuli (1819–1897)—Polish pianist, composer, conductor and teacher—was in a privileged and advantageous position to take into account all that the master brought to his playing and teaching. His in-person account of Chopin's approach to performance—reflected in Mikuli's distinguished editorial contributions to this volume—is invaluable to all who would understand the principles that underlie this body of work.

Mikuli's foreword (in German) was written in 1879 for his landmark edition of Chopin's piano music, originally published by Fr. Kistner, Leipzig. Lamenting the innumerable errors found in earlier French, German and English publications, he sought to provide the reader with a reliable edition based on several sources—especially printed scores corrected in Chopin's own hand; scores in which Mikuli himself noted down the composer's comments during students' lessons; and significant reminiscences by discerning witnesses to Chopin's rare performances.

The following English translation of the original text—lightly edited for the present publication—was first prepared for the 1895 American edition. While markedly shorter than the original, this note touches on all essential issues, concerns and points of view involved in this comprehensive edition.

FOREWORD
Chopin, Pianist and Teacher

by Carl Mikuli

According to a tradition—and, be it said, an erroneous one—Chopin's playing was like that of one dreaming rather than awake—scarcely audible in its continual *pianissimos* and *una cordas,* with feebly developed technique and quite lacking in confidence, or at least indistinct, and distorted out of all rhythmic form by an incessant *tempo rubato!* The effect of these notions could not be otherwise than very prejudicial to the interpretation of his works, even by the most able artists—in their very striving after truthfulness; besides, they are easily accounted for.

Chopin played rarely and always unwillingly in public; "exhibitions" of himself were totally repugnant to his nature. Long years of sickliness and nervous irritability did not always permit him the necessary repose, in the concert hall, for displaying untrammeled the full wealth of his resources. In more familiar circles, too, he seldom played anything but his shorter pieces, or occasional fragments from the larger works. Small wonder, therefore, that Chopin the pianist failed to achieve wide recognition.

Yet Chopin possessed a highly developed technique, giving him complete mastery over the instrument. In all styles of touch the evenness of his scales and passages was unsurpassed—nay, fabulous; under his hands the pianoforte needed to envy neither the violin for its bow nor wind instruments for the living breath. The tones melted one into the other with the liquid effect of beautiful song.

A genuine piano hand, extremely flexible though not large, enabled him to play arpeggios of most widely dispersed harmonies and passages in wide stretches, which he brought into vogue as something never attempted before; and everything without the slightest apparent exertion, a pleasing freedom and lightness being a distinguishing characteristic of his style. At the same time, the tone which he could *draw out* of the instrument was prodigious, especially in the *cantabiles;* in this regard John Field alone could compare with him.

A lofty, virile energy lent imposing effect to suitable passages—an energy without roughness; on the other hand, he could carry away his hearers by the tenderness of his soulful delivery—a tenderness without affectation. But with all the warmth of his peculiarly ardent temperament, his playing was always within bounds, chaste, polished and at times even severely reserved.

In keeping time Chopin was inflexible, and many will be surprised to learn that the metronome never left his piano. Even in his oft-decried *tempo rubato,* one hand—that having the accompaniment—always played on in strict time, while the other, singing the melody, either hesitating as if undecided, or, with increased animation, anticipating with a kind of impatient vehemence as if in passionate utterances, maintained the freedom of musical expression from the fetters of strict regularity.

Some information concerning Chopin the teacher, even in the shape of a mere sketch, can hardly fail to interest many readers.

Teaching was something he could not easily avoid, in his capacity as an artist and with his social attachments in Paris; but far from regarding it as a heavy burden, Chopin dedicated all his strength to it for several hours a day with genuine pleasure. True, his demands on the talent and industry of the pupil were very great. There were often "de leçons orageuses" ("stormy lessons"), as they were called in school parlance, and many a fair eye wet with tears departed from the high altar of the Cité d'Orleans, rue St. Lazare, yet without the slightest resentment on that score against the dearly beloved master. For this same severity, so little prone to easy satisfaction, this feverish vehemence with which the master strove to raise his disciples to his own plane, this insistence on the repetition of a passage until it was understood, were a guaranty that he had the pupil's progress at heart. He would glow with a sacred zeal for art; every word from his lips was stimulating and inspiring. Single lessons often lasted literally for several hours in succession, until master and pupil were overcome by fatigue.

On beginning with a pupil, Chopin was chiefly anxious to do away with any stiffness in, or cramped, convulsive movement of, the hand, thereby obtaining the first requisite of a fine technique: "souplesse" (suppleness), and at the same time independence in the motion of the fingers. He was never tired of inculcating that such technical exercises are not merely mechanical, but claim the intelligence and entire will power of the pupil; and, consequently, that a twentyfold or fortyfold repetition (still the lauded arcanum of so many schools) does no good whatever—not to mention the kind of practising advocated by Kalkbrenner, during which one may also occupy oneself with reading! He treated the various styles of touch very thoroughly, more especially the full-toned *legato*.

As gymnastic aids he recommended bending the wrist inward and outward, the repeated wrist-stroke, the pressing apart of the fingers—but all with an earnest warning against overexertion. For scale practice he required a very full tone, as *legato* as possible, at first very slowly and taking a quicker tempo only step by step, and playing with metronomic evenness. To facilitate the passing under of the thumb and passing over of the fingers, the hand was to be bent inward. The scales having many black keys (B major, F-sharp, D-flat) were studied first, C major, as the hardest, coming last. In like order he took up Clementi's *Preludes and Exercises*,* a work which he highly valued on account of its utility.

According to Chopin, evenness in scale-playing and arpeggios depends not only on the equality in the strength of the fingers obtained through five-finger exercises, and a perfect freedom of the thumb in passing under and over, but foremostly on the perfectly smooth and constant sideways movement of the hand (not *step* by *step*), letting the elbow hang down freely and loosely at all times. This movement he exemplified by a *glissando* across the keys. After this he gave as studies a selection from Cramer's *Études*, Clementi's *Gradus ad Parnassum*, the *Finishing Studies in Style* by Moscheles, which were very congenial to him, Bach's *English* and *French Suites*, and some Preludes and Fugues from the *Well-Tempered Clavier*.

Field's and his own nocturnes also figured to a certain extent as studies, for through them—partly by learning from his explanations, partly by hearing and imitating them as played indefatigably by Chopin himself—the pupil was taught to recognize, love and produce the *legato* and the beautiful connected singing tone. For paired notes and chords he exacted strictly simultaneous striking of the notes, an arpeggio being permitted only where marked by the composer himself; in the trill, which he generally commenced on the auxiliary, he required perfect evenness rather than great rapidity, the closing turn to be played easily and without haste.

For the turn (*gruppetto*) and *appoggiatura*, he recommended the great Italian singers as models: he desired octaves to be played with the wrist-stroke, but without losing in fullness of tone thereby. Only far-advanced pupils were given his *Études,* Op. 10 and Op. 25.

Chopin's attention was always directed to teaching correct phrasing. With reference to wrong phrasing, he often repeated the apt remark that it struck him as if some one were reciting, in a language not understood by the speaker, a speech carefully learned by rote, in the course of which the speaker not only neglected the natural quantity of the syllables, but even stopped in the middle of words. The pseudo-musician, he said, shows in a similar way, by his wrong phrasing, that music is not his mother tongue, but something foreign and incomprehensible to him, and must, like the aforesaid speaker, quite renounce the idea of making any effect upon his hearers by his delivery.

In marking the fingering, especially that peculiar to himself, Chopin was unsparing. Piano-playing owes him many innovations in this respect, whose practicalness caused their speedy adoption, though at first certain authorities, like Kalkbrenner, were fairly horrified by them. For example, Chopin did not hesitate to use the thumb on the black keys, or to pass it under the little finger (with a decided inward bend of the wrist, to be sure), where it facilitated the execution, rendering the latter quieter and smoother. With one and the same finger he often struck two neighboring keys in

*[a portion of the appendix to Muzio Clementi's *Introduction to the Art of Playing on the Piano Forte* (1811, revised ca. 1821)]

viii

succession (and this not simply in a slide from a black key to the next white one), without the slightest noticeable break in the continuity of the tones. He frequently passed the longest fingers over each other without the intervention of the thumb (see *Étude, Op. 10, No. 2*), and not only in passages where (e.g.) it was made necessary by the holding down of a key with the thumb. The fingering for chromatic thirds based on this device (and marked by himself in *Étude, Op. 25, No. 5*) renders it far easier to obtain the smoothest *legato* in the most rapid tempo, and with a perfectly quiet hand, than the fingering followed before. *The fingerings in the present edition are, in most cases, those indicated by Chopin himself* [added italics]; where this is not the case, they are at least marked in conformity with his principles, and therefore calculated to facilitate the execution in accordance with his conceptions.

As for shading, he insisted on a real and carefully graduated *crescendo* and *decrescendo*. On phrasing, and on style in general, he gave his pupils invaluable and meaningful hints and instructions, assuring himself, however, that they were understood by playing not only single passages but whole pieces over and over again, and this with a scrupulous care, an enthusiasm, such as none of his auditors in the concert hall ever had an opportunity to witness. The whole lesson-hour often passed without the pupil's having played more than a few measures, while Chopin, at a Pleyel upright piano (the pupil always played on a fine concert grand, and was obliged to promise to practise on only the best instruments), continually interrupting and correcting, proffered for his admiration and imitation the warm, living ideal of perfect beauty. It may be asserted, without exaggeration, that only the pupil knew Chopin the pianist in his entire unrivalled greatness.

Chopin most urgently recommended ensemble playing, the cultivation of the best chamber music—but only in association with the finest musicians. Whoever could not find such opportunities was urged to seek a substitute in four-hand playing.

With equal insistence he advised his pupils to take up thorough theoretical studies as early as practicable. Whatever their condition in life, the master's great heart always beat warmly for the pupils. A sympathetic, fatherly friend, he inspired them to unwearying endeavor, took unaffected delight in their progress, and at all times had an encouraging word for the wavering and dispirited.

Chopin Masterpieces

Ballade No. 1 in G Minor

Op. 23 (1831–5)

*) The Princess M. Czartorvska, Frau F. Streicher, and Dr F. von Hiller maintain the authenticity of this E♭ in opposition to the D of earlier editions.

Berceuse in D-flat Major
Op. 57 (1843–4)

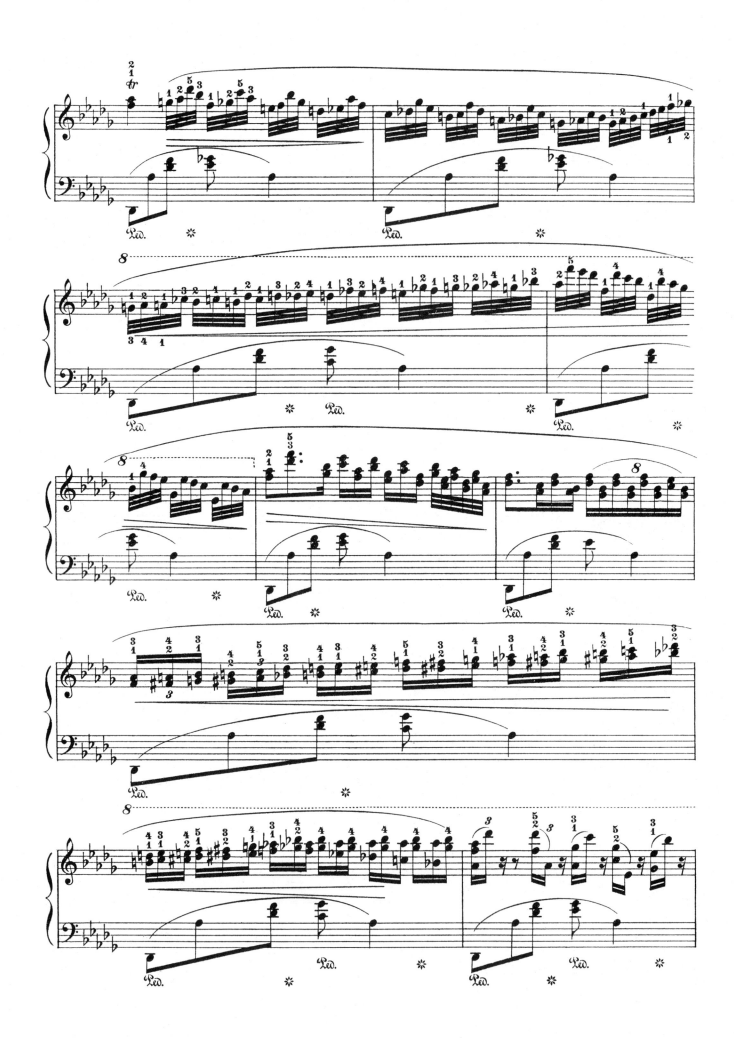

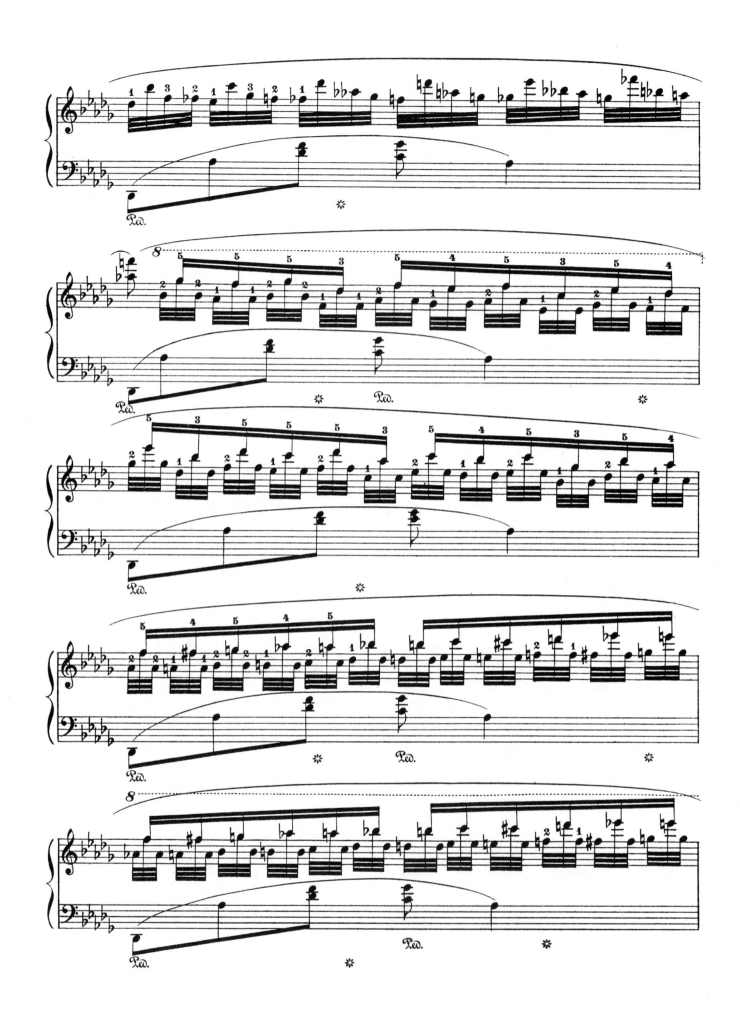

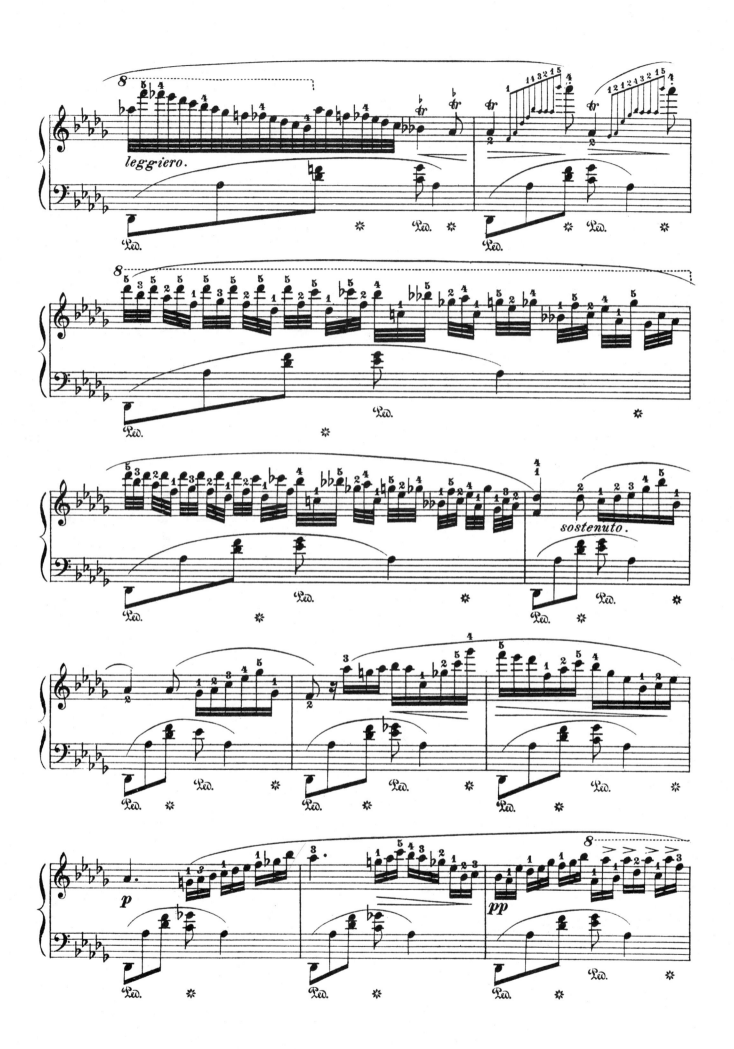

Three Ecossaises

Op. 72, No. 3 (1826)

Etude in C Minor

Op. 10, No. 12 (1830)

Allegro con fuoco. (♩ = 160.)

Etude in E Major
Op. 10, No. 3 (1832)

Etude in G-flat Major

Op. 10, No. 5 (1830)

Etude in G-flat Major

Op. 25, No. 9 (1832–4)

Etude in A-flat Major

Op. 25, No. 1 (1836)

Fantasie-Impromptu
in C-sharp Minor
Op. 66 (1835)

Tempo I.(Allegro agitato.)

Mazurka in B-flat Major

Op. 7, No. 1 (1831)

Mazurka in A Minor

Op. 7, No. 2 (1831)

Mazurka in A Minor
Op. 17, No. 4 (1833)

Mazurka in B Minor

Op. 33, No. 4 (1837–8)

Mazurka in G Minor

Op. 67, No. 2 (1849)

Mazurka in C Major

Op. 67, No. 3 (1835)

Mazurka in A Minor

Op. 68, No. 2 (1827)

Mazurka in F Major
Op. 68, No. 3 (1829)

Marche Funèbre
(1837)

From Sonata No. 2 in B-flat Minor, Op. 35 (1839)

Nocturne in B-flat Minor

Op. 9, No. 1 (1830–31)

Larghetto. (♩ = 116.)

Nocturne in E-flat Major

Op. 9, No. 2 (1830–31)

Nocturne in D-flat Major

Op. 27, No. 2 (1835)

Nocturne in G Minor

Op. 37, No. 1 (1838)

Nocturne in C Minor

Op. 48, No. 1 (1841)

Nocturne in F Minor
Op. 55, No. 1 (1843)

Nocturne in E Minor

Op. 72, No. 1 (1827)

Polonaise in A Major

Op. 40, No. 1 (1838)

Polonaise in F-sharp Minor
Op. 44 (1840–41)

Doppio movimento: (Tempo di Mazurka.)

Polonaise in A-flat Major
Op. 53 (1842)

Prelude in C Major
Op. 28, No. 1

Prelude in A Minor

Op. 28, No. 2

Prelude in E Minor

Op. 28, No. 4

Prelude in B Minor

Op. 28, No. 6

Prelude in A Major

Op. 28, No. 7

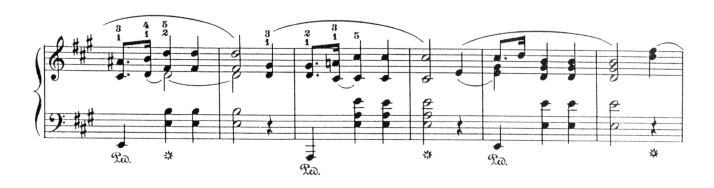

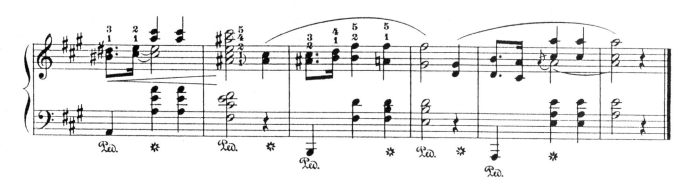

Prelude in D-flat Major

Op. 28, No. 15

Sostenuto.

Prelude in C Minor

Op. 28, No. 20

Prelude in G Minor
Op. 28, No. 22

Molto agitato.

Prelude in D Minor
Op. 28, No. 24

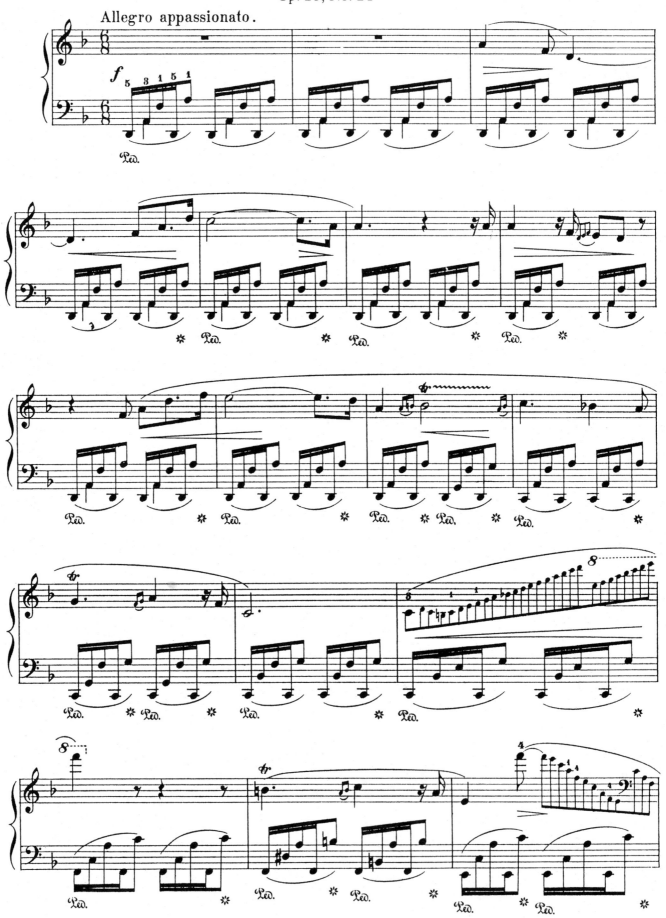

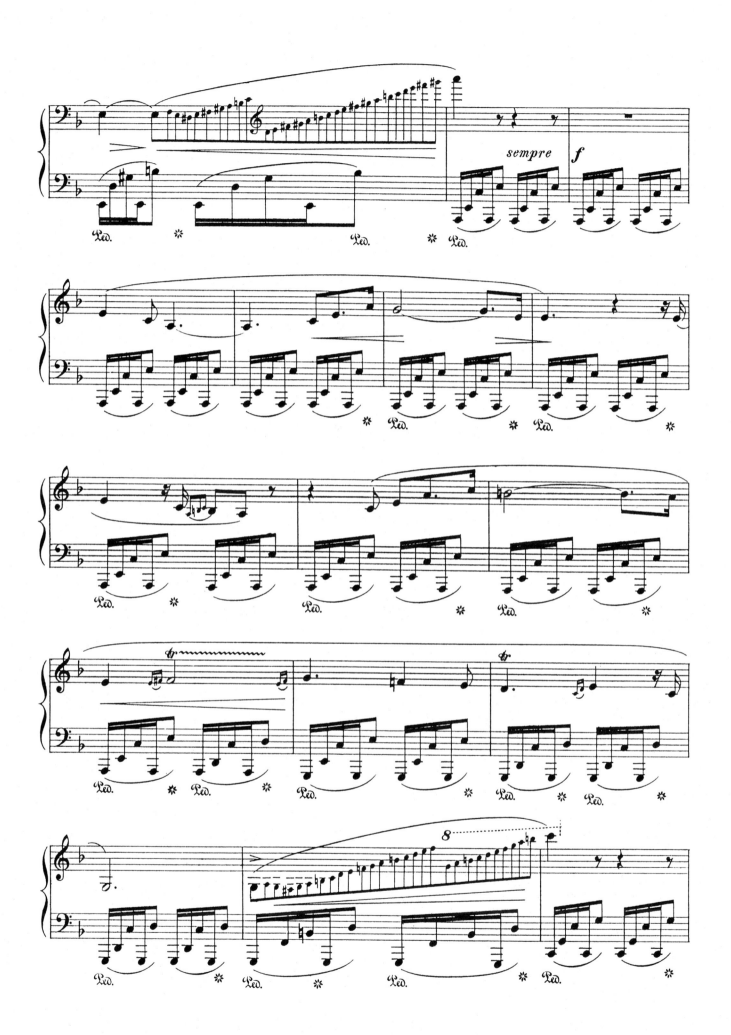

Scherzo No. 2 in B-flat Minor
Op. 31 (1837)

Waltz in E-flat Major
(Grande Valse brillante)
Op. 18 (1831)

Waltz in A Minor
(Grande Valse brillante)
Op. 34, No. 2 (1831)

Waltz in D-flat Major
("Minute Waltz")
Op. 64, No. 1 (1846–7)

Waltz in C-sharp Minor

Op. 64, No. 2 (1846–7)

Più mosso.

Waltz in A-flat Major

("L'adieu")

Op. 69, No. 1 (1835)

Waltz in E Minor

Op. posthumous (1830?)

210   *Waltz, Op. posth.*

END OF EDITION